ISBN 978-1-332-94763-8
PIBN 10441566

1 MONTH OF
FREE
READING

at
www.ForgottenBooks.com

By purchasing this book you are eligible for one month membership to ForgottenBooks.com, giving you unlimited access to our entire collection of over 700,000 titles via our web site and mobile apps.

To claim your free month visit:
www.forgottenbooks.com/free441566

Lyceum Magazine,

MATILDA FLETCHER.

THE SEASON OF 1873-74.

EDITED BY

MARINER J. KENT.

WASHINGTON:
CHRONICLE PUBLISHING COMPANY, 511 NINTH STREET.
1873.

Lyceum Magazine.

MATILDA FLETCHER

WILL LECTURE UPON THE FOLLOWING SUBJECTS:

"MR. GRUMPY,"

"MEN AND THEIR WHIMS,"

"FARMERS' WIVES AND DAUGHTERS,"

(Lecture for Agricultural Societies.)

For terms and dates address

MARINER J. KENT, Agent,
P. O. Box 447, WASHINGTON, D. C

WASHINGTON:
CHRONICLE PUBLISHING COMPANY, No. 511 NINTH STREET.
1873.

PN40
F5
8

LYCEUM MAGAZINE.

MATILDA FLETCHER.

Among the new and successful toilers in the charmed fields of literature none enjoy a wider popularity than Matilda Fletcher. She is characteristically a Western woman, and is aptly called the "Queen of the West" by the critics in that section of the country.

Comparatively unknown in the South and East, except through the columns of the press, her successes at home have already proven beyond a doubt the extraordinary power of her genius, and have marked her as the most promising young speaker in the lecture field.

Born on the frontier, enjoying for years the benefits of farm life, and endowed with a naturally fine physique, she is enabled to bear with impunity the hardships and fatigue incidental to the profession she has chosen.

Commanding and graceful, she presents an appearance on the rostrum second to none. Her voice, clear and sweetly modulated, combined with a ready flow of language and easy, natural gestures, renders her delivery perfect. Entering into the full spirit of her subject, she treats it effectively—often with great feeling, and always with sincere earnestness. She has also the remarkable power of at once engaging the sympathies of her audience, and holding them enchanted and enwrapt with the wit and excellence of her argument to the very close of the lecture. Her manner of speaking extemporaneously, without even a note of reference, also contributes much to the effect of her delivery, and demonstrates that she is a natural and true orator. Hitherto she has confined her lectures entirely to political and reformatory subjects, which she handles with wonderful skill, pleasing the most cultivated audiences, and giving her just fame wherever she presents them. Here new lecture is literary, and entitled "Mr. Grumpy." This is a poem in prose, describing a class of men suggestive of the title, detailing in a pleasant, humorous, and remarkably witty way the characters, hopes, and aspirations of Mr. Grumpy, his failures, the cause of them, and his final regeneration through the power and glory of woman's love. It is delicately satirical, humorous, but never broad; its wit keen and pungent, without being offensive; the follies of men fearlessly exposed, but in a manner that never wounds the most sensitive nature; in fact, the tips of her pointed arrows are so finely ground and discharged with such practiced skill that they reach a vulnerable part without producing a tinge of pain. Withal, the story is charmingly told, with here and there a bit of sentiment or a vein of original poetry, delighting the listener, and rendering the entire lecture a master-piece of intellectual invention. Through the production runs a moral, apparent, but never obtrusive; pointed, but unobjectionable, and inculcating the noblest principles and the most refined morality.

It would not be just to close this article without a tribute to the elevated character, the noble aspirations, and the innate purity of soul that prompt every action and move every impulse in the life of Matilda Fletcher. Struggling through hardships and discouragements, battling against adversity, intent upon reaching the goal placed far beyond the reach of ordinary mortals, the attainment of which will bring power only to be used for the benefit of others, she is, indeed, entitled to all praise and encouragement until she shall have reached that position to which her genius, application, and good womanly qualities so justly entitle her.

M. J. K.

OPINIONS OF THE PRESS.

THE Queen of the Western platform.—*Bulletin, Philadelphia.*

MATILDA FLETCHER delivered two choice lectures to admiring audiences in this place last week. Rarely do we meet with her equal in the lecture field. Many persons present who had heard the most famous "stars" of our nation unhesitatingly declared her efforts superior to them all. A grand future awaits her, and most happy is the audience that shall be privileged to greet her. A soul so noble, a mind so clear, language so chaste, wit and humor so perfectly original, and sparkling with beauty and freshness, or eloquence so entrancing. are rarely, if ever, found so deftly combined in one person. Her lectures are brilliant enough to fill the grandest opera house of the Union, and chaste enough to be heard from the most sacred altars.—*Central Illinoisian, Beardstown, Ill.*

A PERSON of sweet speech and great soul.—*State Register, Des Moines. Iowa.*

SHE possesses a combination of qualities for her profession rarely united in a public speaker, either male or female. She is comely and good to look upon, not by any means the least important consideration, when a majority of her hearers are of the masculine gender. Moreover, she is a brilliant thinker, and impresses her thoughts upon her hearers with all the arts and graces of the most accomplished oratory. Chaste and select in her language, she is still ready in wit and repartee—no interruption ever discomposes her or disturbs her equanimity. But above all other qualifications of this eminent lady for her work, that which commends her most to the sympathy of both sexes is her sincere and earnest love of humanity, her faith in the good that is in every man and woman—a faith so deep that it discovers in every human being, high or low, fortunate or unfortunate,

"Some sacred crypt or altar of a temple
Still vocal with God's laws."
    —*Enterprise, Albert Lea, Minn.*

OUR estimate of the lady is that she is the very Queen of the platform.—*Advertiser, Brownville, Neb.*

MATILDA FLETCHER is a woman of great natural abilities. excellent education, and high culture. She is, indeed, devoted to the work in which she is engaged, and the earnest, eloquent manner in which she advocates her principles would command attention from any audience. Her views are presented with a womanly bearing which wins encomiums from all. She has no ultra measures to propose. Her avowed object is to benefit the race ; to give her sex a true appreciation of the position which woman is entitled to hold. To this she bends all the power of her mind, and the whole-souled sincerity of her nature.—*University Missourian, Columbia, Mo.*

THIS young and gifted speaker fairly enchanted her audience at Milton with her thrilling eloquence.—*Gazette, Janesville, Wis.*

THE lecture of Matilda Fletcher, at Farwell Hall on Wednesday evening, on "Men and Their Whims," was well attended Imagine a form erect, but pliant ; full, but replete with natural grace ; a queenly head, with soft auburn curls clustering over the white classic brow ; eyes whose eloquent fire was blended with a subdued tenderness ; a small, sensitive mouth, the delicate lips of which quivered with the intensity of heartfelt emotion when giving utterance to her belief in what she considers the truth and right; a presence inspired with the spirit of an undaunted but true woman, whose contact with the public has not caused her to lose one particle of womanly delicacy or self-respect—imagine this presence clothed in a plain but flowing robe of black velvet, with but little ornamentation, and you have Matilda Fletcher.—*Gazette, Sterling, Ill.*

NOTWITHSTANDING the almost impassable condition of the roads, and the bad weather, over three hundred persons were assembled at an early hour in the Court House Hall awaiting her appearance. It is useless for us to say that the subject was well handled, and that the lecture made a lasting impression on the minds of the audience. As a lecturer and talented young lady she ranks among the first in the land. —*Sun, Winterset, Iowa.*

THE lecture of Matilda Fletcher on Thursday evening was attended by a large and appreciative audience—in fact, we may say it was the finest assembly of our citizens that has greeted any lecturer during the season. Her subject, "Men and Their Whims," was well chosen, and the brilliant sallies she made and the constant thread of interest running through the lecture kept the audience in good humor with themselves and their entertainer throughout the evening. Matilda Fletcher makes a fine appearance, captivates the audience by her wit, and holds it in her power by the originality of her sentiment, the eloquence, and the genial vein of humor pervading her entire discourse.—*Republican, Kenton, Ohio.*

ELOQUENT in the true meaning of the word.—*Patriot, Chariton, Iowa.*

Special Despatch.]
COLUMBUS. Ohio, March 13.

Matilda Fletcher's lecture at the Opera House to-night was an entire success. The audience was kept in pleased excitement throughout, and as the fair lecturer closed with a glowing picture of that perfect state of society when men and women shall stand together, each aiding the other in a life-work peculiarly fitted to each, there was a spontaneous and prolonged outburst of applause. The lecturer was introduced by Governor Noyes in a few remarks, that were alike honorable to himself and the gifted lady of whom he spoke.—*Gazette, Cincinnati, Ohio.*

SHE kept her audience in good humor, and dismissed them in that frame of mind. —*Press, Washington, Iowa.*

ALTHOUGH it was raining, a very satisfactory and a highly satisfied audience assembled to hear the young lady, who spoke extemporaneously, treated her subject well, and was frequently applauded. Much might be said of her youth, beauty, grace, and all that—but this thing, however charming to look at, is very poor reading. Her lecture was a decided success, in the opinion of the unusually intelligent audience she addressed.—*Journal, Bucyrus, Ohio.*

THE lady spoke without notes, and held the attention of her large audience till the close.—*Commercial, Cincinnati. Ohio.*

THE genius of the lecturer clothed her subject in an instructive and flowery garb. The lady speaks without notes and talks right on from beginning to end without hesitation, and with great fluency.—*Nonpareil, Council Bluffs, Iowa.*

HER delivery is piquant and charming. The audience were much pleased with the evening's entertainment.—*Sentinel, Morrison, Ill.*

"NEMESIS" is the title of the poem delivered by Matilda Fletcher on Wednesday evening. It was listened to by a delighted audience. She is a poet. Perhaps we should say a poetess, to please some captions reader. But call it by whatever name you will, only that we are understood to mean that she has the inspiration of soul which lifts it to a higher plane of thought, and a clearer view of the beautiful, the lovable, and the graceful, in a world ideal and a world natural. Therefore, glittering all over with beautiful coinings of soul-work, and draped with graceful imagery, intoning a wealth of deep poetic sympathy with the pure, the beautiful, the good, that stirs to depths of feeling, and filled full of sweet womanly impulse for the right, is this poem "Nemesis."—*Tribune, Iowa City, Iowa.*

HER reasoning was pellucid, pointed, and unanswerable.—*State Journal, Lincoln, Neb.*

SHE spoke as a woman only can speak, and was listened to with breathless and wrapt attention. Words falling from the lips of a beautiful, noble-souled woman always do good. She is a woman of comprehensive views, a brilliant, argumentative and convincing speaker, and a lady eminently calculated to exert a salutary influence on our national and social affairs.—*Miner, Georgetown, Col.*

NOTWITHSTANDING the extreme cold weather, a good audience assembled at the Opera House last evening to hear the well-known lecturer, Matilda Fletcher. She spoke for an hour and a half with a readiness and eloquence pleasing to her hearers, who manifested their approbation by the most enthusiastic applause. — *Journal, Springfield, Ill.*

MATILDA FLETCHER'S lecture was characteristic of a woman who, possessed of intelligence and resolution, endeavors to rise above the common level of her sex. Deeply impressed with a sense of woman's worth and woman's destiny, she has labored with voice and pen to impart the same feeling to others. A charming manner, united with a commanding presence and rare ability, gives her a power over an audience and secures their sympathy and acquiescence. This was the effect upon those who heard the lady on last Friday evening. Though she spared neither the high nor the low, we had to admit the justice of her criticisms and the point of her witticisms.—*Times, Ashland, Ohio.*

SHE is a lady of surprising eloquence.—*Post, Chicago.*

THE raciest, spiciest address that we have listened to in a long time was delivered on Tuesday evening by Matilda Fletcher. The topic was a grand one, the whole lecture replete with solid matter, touched off with poetic and elocutionary adornments that made it highly enjoyable.—*Republican, Walpello, Iowa.*

THE lecture was listened to with close attention, and received the approval of hearty applause from the audience—*North-West, Ft. Dodge, Iowa.*

A GRACEFUL and fluent speaker, never at a loss for something to say, and her eloquent hits at the whims of social and political life, cut like the blade of Damascus. We hear only one expression from those who attended, and that is that Matilda Fletcher is an agreeable and talented lady, an eloquent and highly entertaining speaker, and a success as a lecturer.—*Eagle, Macomb, Ill.*

OUR people attended the lecture with high expectations, for the lady's fame is great; and if we are to judge by the attention and applause she received, and the congratulations extended to her at the close of the lecture, not one was disappointed. She utters strong words for all the good there is in the world. Her lectures are interspersed with wit, and are not dull in any paragraph.—*Telegraph, Atlantic, Iowa.*

SHE is a pleasant speaker, and may come again.—*Advocate, Green Bay, Wis.*

NOTWITHSTANDING the very inclement weather, the appreciative masses turned out last Tuesday evening to hear Matilda Fletcher, the "Queen of the Western platform." The people gathered at the hall to hear a remarkable woman, and they were not disappointed, for she proved to be all that the press and the public have painted her—young, handsome, and eloquent. Her subject, "Men and Their Whims," was a rich compound of practical sense and humor, and the frequent bursts of applause testified to the high appreciation of the audience. She spoke in a clear, firm voice, cutting right and left the old and young of both sexes, but giving no offence. Her easy, graceful manner at once challenged the admiration of her listeners, and held them to the last.—*Journal, Middletown, Ohio.*

A FEARLESS, forcible, and witty speaker.—*Democrat, St. Anthony, Minn.*

THE Cincinnati *Gazette* closed its report of Matilda Fletcher's address before the General Assembly of Ohio, in the following words: "The address abounded in capital hits throughout, the youth, grace, and beauty of the speaker adding much to the general effect. The hall rang with applause and even those who could not agree with the views of the lecturer professed themselves well pleased with her address."

SHE is very prepossessing in appearance, has a clear, musical voice, and is a speaker of great ability.—*Journal, Madison, Wis.*

MATILDA FLETCHER'S lecture on Friday evening was received with close attention and frequent and hearty applause. A good audience was present, although several protracted meetings were in progress at the time. The lecture, "Men and Their Whims," was full of thought and strong, good sense, yet spiced with happy hits of humor and genuine wit. She speaks without notes, presenting her ideas in a forcible manner, throwing her true womanly soul into the work. She has a sweet, musical voice, a mind of high culture, together with all the genuine elements of oratory.—*Commercial, Danville, Ill.*

THE lecture delivered by Matilda Fletcher at Turner Hall on last evening was undoubtedly the best treat our citizens have had for a long time. She spoke for an hour and a half, and during all that time the audience was so deeply interested that the dropping of a pin on the floor could have been heard, except, when she made some more than usually happy point, she was greeted with hearty applause. * * * She handled her subject, "Men and Their Whims," with a master's skill, and comical as her theme may appear to have been, it showed but little of the comicality when she brought to her aid, in presenting it, the reasoning of a philosopher, the information and patriotism of a statesman, the moral ideas of a true Christian, and the eloquence of a finished orator, and all these qualities embellished by the bewitching smile, artless manner, and true refinement of a beautiful, accomplished, and virtuous woman.—*Marble City News, Cape Girardeau, Mo.*

SHE is an easy, graceful speaker, and thoroughly understands her subject.—*Union, Lockport, N. Y.*

A DEMOCRAT—of the Victor Hugo persuasion—her sympathies are with the toiling masses.—*Sentinel, Newton, Iowa.*

MATILDA FLETCHER lectured on Saturday night at Arcadome Hall to an appreciative and delightful audience. Frank in manner, graceful in elocution, witty, pungent, original in ideas, she entertained her hearers for upward of two hours with a first-class performance. She analyzed the whims of men in a masterly and comprehensive manner, fully vindicating her reputation as one of the first lecturers before the people.—*Republican, Wooster, Ohio.*

KNOWN throughout the West as the Queen of the platform.—*Times, Chicago.*

OUR candid opinion is, that there is not a more entertaining and sensible woman in the lecture field, and our pride in Iowa, we confess, leads us to considerable gratification over her liberal success.—*Journal, Sioux City, Iowa.*

A LADY of genuine eloquence that places her among the most popular of orators.—*Journal, Warrensburg, Mo.*

POSSESSES to an admirable degree the charms of oratory.—*Journal, Sidney, Ohio.*

MATILDA FLETCHER. — This distinguished lady lectured here on Tuesday on "Men and Their Whims." We must confess that the *real* lecture as given by her on the platform differed very materially from the *ideal* formed by us, and after the lecture we no longer wondered at the golden opinions she is winning wherever she goes. Matilda Fletcher is handsome and very graceful, her language pure, and her ideas generally good and original. Her elocution is not quite faultless, and we do not—she's a woman, you know—agree with all her opinions, but as our cotemporary of the *Democrat* said, "she is one of the few women who do not forget their womanhood on the rostrum."—*Republican, Mt. Vernon Ind.*

A LADY of keen intellect, fine voice, and natural grace of manner.—*Post, Rochester, Minn.*

THE lecture at Odd Fellows' Hall on Tuesday night last by Matilda Fletcher was replete with happy hits, keen sarcasm, and unanswerable logic. Her address was clothed in choice language, her manner is graceful, easy, and dignified, and we could but notice the utter absence of those pretentions and vainglorious allusions to self, which so sadly mar the efforts of the majority of speakers. We may add she is young, of charming manners, pleasant features, and as talented as a man of brains, culture, and experience.—*Post, Nashua, Iowa.*

SHE is called the most beautiful woman on the American platform.—*Times, Leavenworth, Kan.*

SHE is a lady of great intelligence, and evinces a thorough acquaintance with the subjects upon which she speaks. All who hear her will be pleased, though they may not endorse her views about many things.—*Statesman, Columbia, Mo.*

PURELY and characteristically a Western girl—a wild rose of the prairie.—*Republican, Kenton, Ohio.*

A POSSESSOR of wit, wisdom, elegance, and beauty.—*Atlas, Monmouth, Ill.*

HER voice is sweet and musical; while her lectures have a happy mingling of pathos, humor, and wit.—*Times, Dubuque, Iowa.*

WE were glad to find on Wednesday evening last so large an audience present to hear Matilda Fletcher on "Men and Their Whims." From an acquaintance with her and hearing her we endorse all the praise the press wherever she has appeared has lavished upon her. Possessed of a cultivated mind, of good figure, an easy and graceful carriage, she makes a commanding appearance on the stage, and by her well-modulated voice and fluent tongue attracts her hearers, keeping them interested throughout her entire lecture. She speaks without notes, and is never at a loss for something to say, and always manages to say that something in the proper place. Her lecture in this city gave entire satisfaction to her hearers, the majority of whom were anxious for her to remain another evening.—*Union, Upper Sandusky, Ohio.*

EVERY sentence drops from her lips as words fitly spoken.—*Republican, Bellefontaine, Ohio.*

A LARGE audience, in point of numbers, quietly awaited the commencement of Matilda Fletcher's lecture at the Opera House last evening, and gave evidence of their willingness and desire to be instructed on "Men and Their Whims," by applauding as soon as she was introduced. She was richly and becomingly attired, is fully self-possessed and graceful before her audience, and in a very pleasing voice, which she controls and modulates finely, she commenced the elaboration of her theme. * * Her lecture was frequently applauded, and was well calculated to incite healthful thought. It was, moreover, richly spiced with humor and incident.—*Observer, Utica, N. Y.*

HER lecture was clothed in the choicest language, bearing plainly the sentiments of a noble woman. She has a very flexible and musical voice, and those who listened to her on Monday night pronounced her the best lady speaker they had ever heard.—*Journal, Omro, Wis.*

THE Congregational Church was fairly filled last evening to hear the lecture of Matilda Fletcher. The audience was, without exception, of our best people, and they listened throughout with wrapt and respectful attention, occasionally manifesting their approval by applause. The speaker's manner and delivery are very pleasant, with ready flow of language and easy, natural gestures, at times manifesting much feeling, and always sincere earnestness. She displayed a wonderful knowledge of the ins and outs; the pipe-laying and the wire-pulling, the trickery, dishonesty, knavery, and corruption of politics. In fact, she is well qualified to hoe her own row as a politician—*Rocky Mountain News, Denver, Col.*

MATILDA FLETCHER'S popularity as a public speaker is well deserved, for she is a woman of rare mental gifts, well-educated, and possesses qualities which fit her in a peculiar manner for success on the rostrum.—*Republic, Genesee, Ill.*

A LARGE and intelligent audience assembled at Klaus' Hall last Friday evening to hear Matilda Fletcher, the popular lady lecturer. She came on the stage alone, modestly, yet confidently, introducing herself to the audience in an exceedingly neat and happy manner. Her subject, "Men and Their Whims," admitted of a wide range, of which she took full advantage. * * * The audience were attentive, and manifested a lively interest. The fair lecturer has a pleasing delivery, and impresses an audience by her quiet dignity and grace of manner and expression. Her utterance is clear and distinct, and at times she is truly eloquent. Above all she is a true womanly woman, and, in the highest sense, adorns the ranks of lady speakers.—*Gazette, Green Bay, Wis.*

MATILDA FLETCHER is one of those ladies who "take to the rostrum," and make the calling a success.—*Press, Mt. Pleasant, Iowa.*

THE most unostentatious, and at the same time the most convincing lecturer that we have ever heard.—*Times, Sioux City, Iowa.*

AS a lecturer she is a decided success.—*Tribune, Afton, Iowa.*

So much has been said of the eloquence and merit of the fair lecturer that we find ourselves at a loss to say anything without repeating that which has found its way into print a hundred times. The lecture as delivered carried the conviction of the audience in its favor, and the applause of all to its author.—*Republican, Keosauqua, Iowa.*

THE lecture of this gifted lady gave the greatest satisfaction. It contained many passages of rare beauty, and was exceedingly well delivered.—*Gazette, Davenport, Iowa.*

MATILDA as a speaker is a success, but as a politician she is inconsistent. She tells a great many truths, and tells them well, and says many funny things in her lecture; and we can truly say that it is well worth listening to.—*Democrat, Lima, Ohio.*

HER correct and impressive elocution enchained the audience; while the fine images, vigorous sentiment, and sharp hits of the lecture elicited deep and unfailing attention.—*Republican. Chicago.*

ALTOGETHER her lecture was a happy hit, and received the merited approbation of her hearers, as attested by frequent rounds of applause.—*Tribune, Denver, Col.*

THE pictures she drew were received with loud applause. She is an easy, graceful speaker, and held the closest attention of her audience till the close of the lecture.—*Union, Junction City, Kansas.*

WE were more than well pleased, and highly entertained. Her voice is sweet and pleasant, and her lecture was delivered with simple gracefulness, without the assumption of any stage airs.—*Journal, Mt. Pleasant, Iowa.*

FOR an hour and a half she held the audience in the profoundest attention; held equally, perhaps, by the grace, fluency, and eloquence of the speaker, and the truths presented.—*Eagle, Vinton, Iowa.*

MATILDA FLETCHER is not afraid to take hold of the evils of the times and handle them in a sensible manner. All she had to say proved most conclusively that she is a woman of good sense.—*Post, Tipton, Iowa.*

2

THE lecture and the lecturer far excelled our anticipations. The subject, "Men and Their Whims," was handled in a manner that attracted the closest attention. The lady is very prepossessing, her language excellent, her manner pleasing.—*Ledger, Canton, Ill.*

SHE is a handsome and talented young lady. Her lecture was received with close attention and applause by the audience, and abounded in good sense, wit, and earnest pathos.—*Press, St. Paul, Minn.*

ALTHOUGH dissenting radically from the sentiment of the most of her lecture, we cannot be blind to her grace, talent, and wit, nor to her uncommon fluency of speech, fine rhetoric, and perfect elocution.—*Patriot, Lansing, Iowa.*

SHE possesses rare gifts, both as a writer and a speaker. To hold an audience as she held hers on last evening might well flatter the most experienced and eminent lecturers.—*Hawkeye, Burlington, Iowa.*

HER lectures are instructive, being highly moral and intellectual. Because of this, and because of the pleasant manner of giving her spicy criticisms, she has gained a high position among lecturers.—*Eagle, Booneville, Mo.*

MATILDA FLETCHER is a close and vigorous thinker, and presents her ideas in an attractive and forcible manner that holds the interest of her audience unabated to the close.—*Register, Whitewater, Wis.*

MATILDA FLETCHER possesses an easy, off-hand manner, more common among Western than among Eastern girls. She has a voice pleasant, not loud, but of singular penetration. She has quite a fund of humor, and is most thoroughly in earnest.—*Herald, Utica, N. Y.*

"MEN and Their Whims" were investigated on Tuesday evening in a thorough and decisive manner. The audience were highly entertained.—*Independent, Brodhead, Wis.*

As a lecturer Matilda Fletcher is certainly favored with rare gifts. Her voice is melodious and sweet, and her manner of speaking is fascinating and pleasing throughout—*Record, Bushnell, Ill.*

HER voice and style of delivery are exceedingly pleasant, and hold the audience in the closest attention.—*Herald, Clinton, Iowa.*

MATILDA FLETCHER, the charming lecturer who spoke at Harlan's Hall on Thursday last, on "Men and Their Whims," gave general satisfaction to every one present. She handles her subject well, and as she becomes interested her lips quiver, showing how deeply she feels many portions of her subject.—*Herald, Marshall, Ill.*

SHE is a fine-looking lady, who delivers her lectures in a witty and pleasing manner, and does not fail to win the sympathies of her audience.—*Banner, Jefferson, Wis.*

MATILDA FLETCHER is one of the most interesting of speakers. Her lectures are full of valuable thought. She is what she has been called a thousand times before—a remarkable woman. She is young, but she has read and thought more than two-thirds of the men who are twice her age.—*Excelsior, Moquoketa, Iowa.*

HER lecture was listened to with great attention. She is a pleasant and agreeable speaker.—*Independent, Kewanee, Ill.*

EVERY man and woman in the country knows the facts of her relating; but the eloquent and earnest style in which she addresses her hearers, stamps her at once as a lady of no ordinary gifts. Her grace, ease, and fluency of speech enlist and enchain her auditory.—*Commonwealth, Topeka, Kan.*

SHE speaks extemporaneously, and with an ease and eloquence seldom achieved by our ablest speakers.—*Herald, Richmond, Ind.*

MATILDA FLETCHER'S style of speaking as she grows interested in her topic is far better than one would anticipate. All who went were delighted with her original and unique manner of address and her peculiarly fresh and cutting witticisms. To say that we were well pleased does not suffice; nothing in the line of lectures, speeches, or oratory ever delivered in this place gave such perfect and general satisfaction.—*Messenger, Atlantic, Iowa.*

MATILDA FLETCHER possesses the rare combination of good sense, eloquence, pathos, and humor—together with an elegance of delivery very seldom met with in lady speakers. We predict for this gifted lady lecturer a bright future, and the reward of those who, seeing their duty, dare faithfully to perform it.—*Herald, Plattsmouth, Neb.*

A LADY of most engaging manners, excellent education, brilliant talent, and purity of thought and expression.—*Press, Iowa City.*

MATILDA FLETCHER is witty—quaintly so at times, fearlessly and independently logical—never hesitating to use the scalpel to political sores, and combines, withal, a winsome and simple style of prompt, rippling, sparkling oratory, which, joined to her own charms of person irresistibly carries her audience along with her.—*Press, La Salle, Ill.*

SHE is witty and sarcastic at times, and in all one of the most pleasing and entertaining speakers we ever heard.—*Register, Canton, Ill.*

THOSE of our citizens who failed to hear this lady last evening missed a rare treat, indeed. Pure and lofty in character, her sentiments evidently were the expressions of a noble woman. Easy and graceful in movement, becoming, and even prepossessing, in appearance, she won the enthusiastic admiration of her audience.—*Journal, Lockport, N. Y.*

SHE has a finely modulated voice, speaks unhesitatingly, and sends her ringing sentences right and left, regardless of the set notions of any party.—*Gazette, Champaign, Ill.*

THE lecture of Matilda Fletcher on Thursday evening was reasonably well patronized. Her subject was "Men and Their Whims." She handled it well, and elicited considerable applause. She is quite pretty and graceful. She speaks fluently, using none but the best language. Her gestures are graceful, and her style pleasing and easy. We understand she has been engaged for another lecture, and will be here again next month.—*Messenger, Marshall, Ill.*

FOR an hour and a half she held her audience in the closest attention. Her style is a high finish of elocution, her story a mingling of humor, good sense and pathos. Her manner is one of ease and culture, and is aided by the rare and valuable gift of a voice marvellously flexible and musical.—*Courier, Ottumwa, Iowa.*

HER lecture was replete with logical fact, solid sense, and truths, which had a telling effect upon those present. She is exceedingly pleasant and engaging in her manner, and her personal appearance very prepossessing and attractive.—*Tribune, Lawrence, Kan.*

MATILDA FLETCHER is one of the pleasantest speakers we have ever listened to; language faultless, while her subjects are always well chosen.—*Tribune, Fremont, Neb.*

THE lecture on Monday evening fully sustained the reputation of the speaker as a graceful and eloquent lecturer.—*Plaindealer, Fort Madison, Iowa.*

HER arguments are presented in a forcible style. She is affable, and will make hosts of friends wherever she may go.—*Banner, Black River Falls, Wis.*

THE lecture was full of thought and strong in good sense ; while from beginning to end it glittered with a continuous sparkle of beautiful ideas and exquisite sentiment. Her rich, musical voice and earnestness of manner held the undivided attention of the audience.—*State Register, Des Moines, Iowa.*

SHE is by far the best female speaker we ever listened to. She has a finely modulated voice, and speaks unhesitatingly and forcibly.—*Transcript, Golden, Col.*

WE have heard many of the noted public speakers of the country, and can unhesitatingly give her a place in the front ranks.—*Standard, Waukon, Iowa.*

SHE speaks as one having a mission to fulfil—a high purpose—and no one can doubt that the world would be better if her suggestions were heeded. Altogether it is impossible to convey an adequate idea of the excellence of the lecture. All who were present were charmed with the eloquence of the handsome lecturer.—*Messenger, Mexico, Mo.*

IT is no undue praise to say that it was good, because brimful of truth, and excellent, because delivered in so pleasing a manner.—*Gazette, Cedar Falls, Iowa.*

THE principal charm of this young lady's lecture is that she uses no ranting style of argument, but speaks with spice and rich humor. Her wit is genuine, and of high character. She is a young, beautiful, and accomplished lady.—*Tribune, Minneapolis.*

IN personal appearance she is prepossessing and attractive, fine form, beautiful features, a rich, clear voice, and easy and graceful in all her movements. To say that her lecture was a complete success would be to express but a feeble comment upon its merit.—*Gazette, Mt. Carroll, Ill.*

MATILDA FLETCHER AS A POLITICAL SPEAKER.

Matilda Fletcher's popular lectures disclosed such a thorough knowledge of men and measures in the political world; such a true idea of reform and hearty appreciation of justice, that her services were eagerly sought by the State Central Committees during the last Presidential campaign. She devoted three months and a half to the cause of Republicanism, divided her time among seven States, and was received everywhere with enthusiasm. The following are a few of the encomiums bestowed during her succession of brilliant triumphs:

BROWNVILLE.
Associated Press Despatch.]

BROWNVILLE, Neb., July 16.

Matilda Fletcher delivered an address in this city last night to an immense audience in defence of the Administration. It was an able address, and was enthusiastically received.

[From the Brownville Advertiser.]

On last Monday evening such a forensic effort as never before emanated from McPherson Hall was delivered by Matilda Fletcher. The hall was full of Republicans, Democrats, and "What is it?" together with a large number of ladies, all of whom were richly repaid for their presence.

* * * * * * *

But the time will not permit a more extended epitome. Suffice it to say the address fascinated all who sympathized with her views, and elicited from the Opposition encomiums as to her power as a speaker. Our own estimation of the lady is, that she is the very Queen of the platform. In style she is fearless, forcible, and witty, and she is endowed with keen intellect, musical voice, natural grace of manner, with face and form perfect in lineament and symmetry. We sincerely hope she will find it convenient to visit us again.

[From the Tecumseh (Neb.) Chieftain, July 20.]

Last Monday evening we were in the city of Brownville, and were more than delighted with our good luck in being in the city on the same evening that Matilda Fletcher

was to address the people. McPherson's large hall was crowded with ladies and gentlemen to hear the distinguished lady orator speak in defence of General Grant. We had only heard of this gifted lady, but had no idea of her eloquence and the masterly style with which she handles her subject. We have heard many able speeches in that hall, but that of Matilda Fletcher's surpassed them all in beauty of diction, easy address, distinct articulation, vivacity, earnestness of purpose, and finished propositions. Her audience was intelligent, appreciative, and very often interrupted the speaker by prolonged rounds of applause.

We might have objected to the employment of a lady to make a political speech, but after we heard Matilda Fletcher we "gave it up," and can vouch that her speeches are most effective, and calculated to do good wherever she speaks or lectures, and those who can secure her services on the rostrum will be well satisfied. When you hear Matilda Fletcher you will hear a good-looking, modest, pleasant-voiced, intellectual, well-educated lady.

LINCOLN.
[From the Lincoln State Journal.]

Representative Hall was crowded last evening by an enthusiastic and appreciative audience, who came to hear the political issues of the day discussed from a lady's standpoint.

Matilda Fletcher is a lady young in years, but she has already established a national reputation. Her address is earnest and pleasing, her voice is peculiarly clear and distinct, but rich and full in tone, and she reasons a case like a lawyer who disdains to stoop to claptrap or sensationalism.

* * * * * * *

She was constantly and heartily applauded, and it is agreed upon all sides that her speech was the ablest and most convincing of all that the present political campaign has called forth in our city.

PLATTSMOUTH.
Associated Press Despatch.]

PLATTSMOUTH, Neb., July 25.

Matilda Fletcher spoke to a crowded

house last night in behalf of Grant and Wilson, taking the argument that we crucify our Presidents on the cross of patronage.

[From the Plattsmouth Herald.]

Matilda Fletcher spoke to an intelligent and appreciative audience last night in Fitzgerald's Hall. The lady is of fine personal appearance, dresses in good taste, (so the ladies said,) and is very graceful on the platform. So much for herself, and now for

HER SPEECH.

* * * * * * *

Her speech was a fine effort, whether viewed from a literary or political standpoint, and her earnest, effecti.e manner, must have convinced all that she believed what she said, and had thoroughly investigated her subject. She was repeatedly cheered, and altogether it was the most enthusiastic meeting we have held as well as the best and strongest speech of this season.

OMAHA.

Special Telegram to the Inter-Ocean, Chicago.]

OMAHA, Neb., July 26.

Matilda Fletcher spoke last night in Redick's Opera House to an immense audience. Every one appeared to be well entertained and highly pleased with her speech.

[From the Omaha Tribune and Republican.]

At 8 o'clock Redick's Opera House was filled to an uncomfortable degree with ladies and gentlemen who had been attracted thither by the announcement that a woman —a real, live, handsome, witty, and wise one—was to deliver an address upon the political issues of the day.

As soon as the lucky portion of the audience had found seats, and the unlucky standing room, Matilda Fletcher stepped gracefully forward on the platform, and was introduced to the assemblage by Dr. Benjamin, president of the Central Grant and Wilson Club. She was attired in a neatly-fitting and highly-becoming dress of some white material, but of just what kind our ignorance of such matters prevents us saying. The audience at once recognized her as a woman of medium height, good form, and of handsome and expressive features.

* * * * * * *

Throughout her address she was warmly applauded, and although we should be pleased to, yet we do not expect to see during this campaign another audience as well entertained and highly pleased as was the one last night.

She has a wonderfully sweet and very powerful voice, it seeming no exertion whatever for her to speak rapidly and yet reach the ear of the most distant auditor.

Upon the part of the Omaha Republicans we can assure all whom it may concern that her address last night was in every particular an able and successful one, and certain to result in great good to the Republican cause. Whatever doubt that might have been previously entertained by some of our people as to the policy of having a political speech from a woman, was effectually and happily removed by the test.

[From the Omaha Bee.]

The simple announcement that the political issues of the hour were to be discussed at Redick's Opera House by a lady, had th. effect of filling the large lecture room in that building to its utmost capacity at a very early hour last evening. Fully one-half of that large audience was composed of ladies, which must have been a most gratifying sight to the lectures as she made her appearance upon the stage. Dr. Benjamin, president of the Central Grant and Wilson Club, had the pleasure of introducing Matilda Fletcher to the assemblage.

* * * * * *

The fair speaker was listened to throughout with the deepest attention by all, and it was the universal opinion that Matilda Fletcher had more than filled our expectations. She is possessed of all the qualities that go to make an effective speaker—eloquence, wit, logic, originality, and beauty, and wherever she goes she is bound to meet with success.

PERU.

Special Telegram to the Inter-Ocean, Chicago.]

LA SALLE, Ill., August 2.

Matilda Fletcher, of Iowa, addressed the people of Peru last evening, and in a speech distinguished by historical research and great eloquence, defended the Administration. It was a thorough refutation of the charges brought against the President by his enemies, and was received with great enthusiasm.

COUNCIL BLUFFS.
Associated Press Despatch.]

COUNCIL BLUFFS, Iowa, August 10.

The Republicans held a large and enthusiastic meeting here to-night to rejoice over the result of the North Carolina election. Guns were fired, and Matilda Fletcher delivered an able and eloquent address, which was well received.

[From the Council Bluffs Nonpareil]

The ablest, most interesting, instructive, eloquent, and sensible speech ever listened to by a Council Bluffs audience was delivered by Matilda Fletcher last evening. Having just returned from an extended tour for a day's rest, arrangements for the delivery of her address last night were not made until late in the afternoon. However, as soon as the consent of the gifted lady was obtained, it became noised throughout the city that she was to deliver her address upon Grant and his traducers, and an hour before the time for which the meeting was called found the large and commodious hall filled to its utmost capacity.

At 8 o'clock the fair speaker entered the densely packed hall amid the greatest enthusiasm, and shortly thereafter was introduced to the expectant audience as the speaker of the evening.

* . *   *   *   *   *

Her whole address was characterized by good logic and equally good sense, and abounded in telling hits and salient points. Altogether, it was the greatest success of the season . Those who were not present missed a treat which they could ill afford to lose. They are indeed fortunate who are privileged to hear this truly eloquent speaker. Not one in the field can show a more thorough knowledge of the political status of the Presidential candidates now before us, and of the men who are the leaders of the contest on both sides. Nor have we ever been able to hear as convincing an address from the lips of any speaker, male or female. Her immense audience listened with eager interest to every syllable.

[From the Council Bluffs Republican.]

The meeting at the Court-house on Saturday evening was the largest and most enthusiastic held in this city during the campaign. But few hours were allowed in which to advertise that the able and accomplished lady, Matilda Fletcher, would address the Grant and Wilson Club meeting, but the time proved sufficient to try the capacity of our largest hall.

At an early hour every seat was occupied, and before the speaking commenced there was not standing room to be had. The wide reputation of the speaker was well known by the residents of this city, and all crowded, eager to hear her handle the subject of which she must be acknowledged mistress. As a political speaker Matilda Fletcher stands at the head of American women.

ATLANTIC.
[From the Atlantic Telegraph, August 14.]

Matilda Fletcher spoke in this city last night to a large audience, holding their attention for two hours. We have not time to-day to make anything like a full report of the address. It was the most logical, most effective political address ever delivered in this town or will be during the campaign. The lady left this morning for Ohio, being booked for an address at Columbus, August 22, and for a two weeks' campaign in that State. She will help the cause more than any other speaker in that grand old State.

MUSCATINE.
Associated Press Despatch.]

MUSCATINE, Iowa, August 17.

Matilda Fletcher addressed an immense campaign meeting at the Opera House in this city last evening in an eloquent plea for Grant.

[From the Muscatine Journal.]

Whatever may be the opinions or prejudices of our citizens concerning the vexed question of women appearing in public, especially in the capacity of political speakers, certain it is that appearances last evening, on the occasion of Matilda Fletcher's address on the political issues of the hour, did not indicate that they look upon the question with disfavor.

Olds' Opera House, where the fair speaker appeared, was crowded to its utmost capacity—which is, in effect, saying that the audience numbered at least one thousand people, and was probably the largest in-door assemblage ever known in this city. It consisted of the most intelligent classes, and the ladies, if anything, predominated.

Promptly at the appointed hour she appeared upon the stage, and was introduced by J. S. Hatch, Esq. Neatly attired in white, of medium height, and with a good form, pleasing and expressive features, and a graceful manner, the audience could not fail to be at once favorably impressed with her.

* * * * * * *

She was listened to throughout with the most wrapt attention, and was frequently interrupted by tumultuous applause, inspired by her happy hits and telling truths. All who heard her could not fail to be impressed with her eloquence and earnestness and we believe that her logic, if it did not overcome the prejudices of some who did not agree with her, at least made a good many conversions.

COLUMBUS.

Associated Press Despatch.]

COLUMBUS, Ohio, August 22.

Matilda Fletcher, of Iowa, delivered an able and eloquent address to-night in the Athenæum, under the auspices of the Grant and Wilson Club. Her audience was large and enthusiastic.

Special Despatch to the Cincinnati Gazette.

COLUMBUS, Ohio, August 22.

One of the most successful meetings held in this city for a long time was the one held at the Athenæum to-night, under the auspices of the Grant Club. The house was packed with an enthusiastic audience of our best citizens, including very many ladies. The meeting was called to order by General Knapp, who introduced Matilda Fletcher, of Iowa, as the speaker of the evening.

She was dressed in pure white, and looked like what she is—a sensible woman. She spoke for two hours, holding the attention of the audience from first to last, and drawing frequent outbursts of applause.

[Here follows an outline of her address, which is omitted.]

Special Despatch to the Cincinnati Commercial.

COLUMBUS, Ohio, August 22.

* * * * * * *

The speech was excellently received, and cheer after cheer demonstrated the satisfaction of the large and well-behaved audience.

[From the Columbus State Journal.]

A large audience, in which there were many ladies, gathered at the Athenæum last night to hear Matilda Fletcher, of Iowa, who delivered an address under the auspices of the Republican Club. The audience had the appearance of being one of the most intelligent that ever assembled in "Old Drury," and although there was a marked exhibition of interest and much cheering, there was an air of proper deportment about the meeting that gave an impression to the observer different from that usually gained in the political fray. In short, it is only fair to say that the gathering was a select affair in politics.

* * * * * * *

The address closed with an eloquent tribute to the President, which set the audience into a thunder of applause; indeed, the very many demonstrations of favor throughout the address denoted a warm, hearty reception, that must have been very encouraging to the lady herself, as well as to those who invited her to visit this city.

LONDON.

Special Despatch to the Cincinnati Gazette.]

LONDON, Ohio, August 24.

Matilda Fletcher addressed one of the largest and most enthusiastic Republican meetings here to-night that we have ever had. Every inch of Toland Hall was occupied, many being compelled to stand during the entire address. Very many ladies attended the meeting, and showed an interest and enthusiasm rarely seen. She spoke over two hours, and if President Grant was never before vindicated, most surely it was done by Matilda Fletcher this evening, and in the fairest dispositioned and most convincing address yet given by any orator on the stump. She substantiated her assertions and arguments at every step by proof that cannot be denied, nor did they fall on barren soil. Many Democrats and probably Liberals, if we have any in London, were in the hall, and listened with much interest, and perhaps some conviction. We should be glad to have this Western star visit the Eastern States, where, if more need her voice for the truth and right, it would do so much. Our people pronounce Matilda Fletcher the best female orator on the American platform.

URBANA, OHIO.
[From the Citizen and Gazette.]

The first regular meeting of the Urbana Grant and Wilson Club was held at the City Hall on Monday evening, (August 26.) The attendance was large, the hall being well filled with ladies and gentlemen. The meeting was addressed by Matilda Fletcher, of Iowa, who fully sustained the high reputation she has secured as a public speaker.

*   *   *   *   *   *

The address was well received by the audience and the speaker frequently applauded. She is well posted in regard to the political affairs of the country, and but few public speakers of the sterner sex excel her in the pleasing and forcible style in which she presents her views to the public. She will make a favorable impression wherever she speaks.

BELLEFONTAINE, OHIO.
[From the Republican.)

Matilda Fletcher had a splendid audience Tuesday night, (August 27.) The meeting for her was announced for her only the day before, but Opera Hall was crowded, and a number of ladies took seats on the stage with the speaker. The audience listened to her for more than two hours, giving her the closest attention, and greeting her with frequent and hearty demonstrations of applause. Her happy hits were highly enjoyed. The speech was eloquent, witty, and argumentative. Everybody speaks in its praise, and many say that it was the best they ever heard. No wonder Iowa rolls up such tremendous Republican majorities when she has such eloquent champions of the truth.

FINDLAY.
Special Despatch to the Cleveland Leader.]

FINDLAY, Ohio, August 29.

Matilda Fletcher is addressing a very large and enthusiastic audience, of both parties and sexes, at Wheeler's Hall, which is crowded to its utmost capacity. She holds her hearers spell bound with her eloquence. Her finely-rounded periods and well-taken points are telling grandly for the cause. Her fine appearance and modest manner, as well as her thrilling and matchless eloquence, rivet the attention, and fairly carry the hearts, of her hearers by storm. Her visit will do the cause of Republicans much good.

ELYRIA.
Special Despatch to the Cincinnati Gazette.]

ELYRIA, Ohio, September 3.

Matilda Fletcher, of Iowa, spoke to a large audience, at Town Hall, last evening, in behalf of Grant and Wilson. At least one thousand people were present, and large numbers were unable to get even standing room in the hall. Her speech was a complete vindication of Grant and his administration. She spoke for two hours, holding her entire audience to the last. She was applauded throughout.

[From the Elyria Independent Democrat.]

At 7 o'clock on Monday evening, (September 2,) the new Grant gun thundered forth ten rounds, as a signal for the meeting, to hear Matilda Fletcher, of Iowa, speak in behalf of Grant and Wilson. The people were there en masse, and long before she appeared upon the stage the Town Hall was densely packed with citizens, male and female, and many could not gain admission. She was introduced by S. W. Baldwin, president of the Grant Club, and was greeted with hearty applause. She is young, with round, plump features, light, wavy hair, has keen, sharp eyes, and, as the sequel proved, has a mind gifted with great power, and tongue and voice capable of making that power felt to an extent rarely witnessed among men. She spoke for two hours, and scarcely one of the great throng left their sitting or standing position until she finished her speech. It was the best and most effective campaign speech that has been delivered in Elyria. Her logic was plain and irresistible; now dealing with stern facts, now appealing to the sound reason of her hearers, and then showing the ridiculous position of Greeley and the Democracy most triumphantly, by *reductio ad adsurdum*. We have only room to say further that the Republican party and its nominees have not a more effective champion than Matilda Fletcher.

FREEPORT.

Special Telegram to the Inter-Ocean, Chicago.]

FREEPORT, Ill., September 10.

The Republicans of this city gave a rousing reception to Matilda Fletcher this evening at Wilcoxon's Opera House. Every inch of space was filled; her speech was able and eloquent.

[From the Carroll County, (Ill.,) Mirror.]

We had the pleasure of listening to Matilda Fletcher, the eloquent Iowa orator, at Freeport, on Tuesday night. Her reception at Freeport was very flattering. Wilcoxon's Opera House has never been so crowded; fully twelve hundred people were in the hall; the best class of citizens composed the audience, many of whom were ladies.

She spoke for an hour and forty minutes, and the hall was fuller, if possible, at the close than when she commenced. The greater part of her time was devoted to the defence of the President, both in his private and official capacity. Her speech was a series of telling points—as one gentleman afterwards remarked : " It was full of points "—in favor of Grant and the Republican party.

* * * * * *

She was frequently interruped by the applause of the audience, which, at times, was difficult to suppress, to allow her to proceed.

MONMOUTH.

[From the Monmouth (Ill.) Atlas.]

MONMOUTH, Ill., September 11.

The Republican meeting in this city on Wednesday evening was a great success. Our citizens turned out *en masse* to witness the parade of tanners and young ladies, and hear Matilda Fletcher's address. The young ladies, about forty in number, all appeared in regulation uniform, white dresses, blue capes, pink hats, and handsome faces, each

3

carrying a transparency inscribed with the names of Grant and Wilson.

* * * * * * *

The hall was occupied to its full capacity, the ladies attending in force, and four of their number occupying the platform with the president.

The speaker's prepossessing appearance could hardly have failed to make a good impression and open the way for a favorable reception of her address. She is a very modest and ladylike person, with round and handsome features, a remarkably strong but not masculine voice, and an unusually clear utterance.

* * * * * * *

The interest of her address is attested by the attention she received from the audience for nearly two hours, and the fact is established that a woman can talk politics without defiling her lips or offending good taste.

QUINCY.

Special Despatch to the St. Louis Globe.]

QUINCY, Ill., September 12.

Matilda Fletcher delivered an address tonight at the Opera House on Grant and his traducers. The house was densely packed, not even standing room being obtainable, and hundreds were unable to get in. Many ladies were present. The lecturer kept the immense audience spell-bound over two hours with the burning eloquence of her vindication of the hero, patriot, and statesman, U. S. Grant, which was grand beyond description. No speech of the campaign has had the effect that this one will have.

Special Despatch to the Missouri Democrat.]

QUINCY, Ill., September 12.

Matilda Fletcher delivered her famous lecture at the Opera House this evening, before an immense audience, among whom was a large number of Democrats and Liberals. She was listened to with the closest attention for two hours, her laughing sarcasm and many telling hits eliciting great applause. At the close she was greeted with three rousing cheers.

Special Despatch to the Inter-Ocean, Chicago.]

QUINCY, Ill., September 12.

Matilda Fletcher spoke to the largest political gathering of the campaign, at the

Opera House last night, on Grant and his traducers. The auditorium, galleries, boxes, aisles, and every foot of room was densely packed. She held her immense audience for nearly two hours, and her finely-rounded periods, well taken points, are telling grandly ; her modest manners, as well as her thrilling and matchless eloquence, unite the attention and fairly carry the hearts of all her hearers by storm.

[From the Quincy Daily Whig.]

The largest political meeting of the campaign was held last evening at the Opera House, the occasion being the lecture by Matilda Fletcher on Grant and his traducers. The Opera House was crowded to its utmost capacity. Parquet, dress circle, galleries, boxes, aisles, and every available space and standing room were completely filled, the immense audience remaining spell-bound for nearly two hours by the eloquent and patriotic lady.

*　　*　　*　　*　　*　　*　　*

DANVILLE.
Special Despatch to the St. Louis Globe.]

DANVILLE, Ill., September 14.

Matilda Fletcher, the lady orator of Iowa, spoke last night to a very large and enthusiastic audience. Although the hall was literally packed, and the speech was just two hours long, there was no diminution in the interest. Her style is dignified, her language pure, and her ability to talk wonderful. She uses no " notes," her speeches being entirely impromptu. Her speeches are purely political, no sentimentalism, but good, strong political doctrines. She is possessed of a good deal of magnetism, has a pleasant, rippling laugh, and is quite pretty. The people were well pleased.

Special Telegram to the Inter-Ocean, Chicago.]

DANVILLE, Ill., September 14.

Matilda Fletcher spoke here last night on the political issues of the day. The hall was completely filled. Her speech lasted just two hours. She held the audience spell-bound throughout. She has a wonderful flow of language, a fine, musical voice, and a clear and distinct understanding of the political issues. Her reception here was flattering beyond description.

[From the Danville Commercial.]

On Friday night the Grant Club was addressed by Matilda Fletcher, of Iowa, in a most agreeable and eloquent manner. The hall was full to its utmost capacity. The lady was escorted to the hall by the Tanners, and led by Prof. Reynold's Silver Cornet Band. She is a woman of vast information, and has a flow of most elegant and terse language, so that her speech is full of eloquence and passion.

As a political speech it was a success. But few of our ablest speakers could go over the political history of the country with the alacrity and address that she did. Her spirit and tone was most excellent. She has no bitterness, but speaks the truth in love as a general thing; once in a while a flow of the bitter is perceptible. The best wishes of the people follow her. If she comes again the hall will not hold the audience.

MATTOON.
Special Despatch to the Inter-Ocean, Chicago.]

MATTOON, Ill., September 16.

Matilda Fletcher drew an immense crowd here to-night. She spoke in the largest hall in the city, which was densely packed, and hundreds were turned away, unable to gain admittance. Her speech of full two hours' duration was the most able, entertaining, and exhaustive refutation of the charges against President Grant, and the clearest vindication of the Administration made here during the campaign. She is a powerful and attractive speaker, and hurls her keen shafts of wit and trenchant criticism in a fearless and exceedingly womanly manner.

[From the Tri-Weekly Mattoon Journal.]

One of the very largest and the finest and best Republican mass meetings of the campaign took place last night on the occasion of the novelty of the day—a " stump speech " from a lady. The largest hall in the city was packed to its utmost capacity, every nook and corner being occupied, and yet hundreds could not gain even standing room. Hundreds stood through the whole two hours and a quarter of the speech in the aisles and all over the rear of the hall. Although the audience was dense and promiscuous, the most perfect order prevailed, and the behavior was model. The meeting was a most splendid success in every respect, its great and crowning glory being the eloquent, convincing, and silvery torrent of womanly speech by the fair stump speaker.

[From the Mattoon Gazette.]

As soon as the shades of night began to gather the crowd commenced pouring into the hall, and by 7 o'clock it was well filled, and before the speaker came in was crowded to overflowing, so that persons yet coming were told there was no room; but anxiety to hear gave hope, and they crowded in, filling the platform, aisles, and vestibule, which were packed almost to suffocation We never before saw so many persons in the hall, and it has often been crowded. * * * We have known that her speeches were well received wherever she has been, and that the press has paid her the tribute of liberal praise; but we confess we did not comprehend the completeness and ability with which she discusses the questions of the day until we had the pleasure of hearing her ourselves.

TERRE HAUTE.

Special Despatch to the St. Louis Globe.]

TERRE HAUTE, Ind., September 17.

Matilda Fletcher, the brilliant and beautiful advocate of Republicanism, is addressing a mammoth audience at the Wigwam to-night. Great numbers who went there to hear her were forced to leave, being unable to get within hearing distance, so great is the general curiosity to see and the anxiety to hear her. All this rush to hear her, and Lent's circus and the Abbott pantomimists performing in the city at the same time. She creates a good impression, and is womanly and reserved.

[From the Terre Haute Express.]

One of the few positively immense popular demonstrations that have marked the progress of this campaign was that of last evening, on the occasion of Matilda Fletcher's appearance in this city to advocate the claims of the Republican party and its candidates. The Wigwam and adjacent grounds were crowded; hundreds left because they

could not find standing room within hearing of the speaker.

* * * * * * *

She is an effective speaker, an earnest, impassioned orator. She spoke more than two hours, and kept alive the interest of her immense audience to the very last. She was frequently interrupted by outbursts of applause.

MUNCIE.

Special Despatch to the Cincinnati Gazette.]

MUNCIE, Ind., October 5.

Matilda Fletcher, of Iowa, spoke here to-night to a crowded house, and aroused by her eloquence, wit, and telling hits intense enthusiasm. She spoke two hours and ten minutes, in vindication of General Grant against the calumnies of designing men. She has the martyr's tongue and statesman's thought. At the conclusion of her speech she was surrounded by those of her own sex and complimented by all. The meeting is regarded as a grand success, and productive of much good, while she has made a reputation in Indiana that will endure.

EAST SAGINAW.

[From the Enterprise, East Saginaw, Michigan.]

The rink last evening was filled to listen to Matilda Fletcher, the eloquent Western lady orator. In the audience could be seen a goodly number of ladies, and although the air was extremely chilly throughout the entire evening, the speaker commanded the strictest attention during the entire delivery of her speech, being frequently interrupted by cheers. Her speech savored considerably of sarcasm, was pithy, to the point, and well received. * * *

BURLINGTON.

Associated Press Despatch.]

BURLINGTON, Iowa, October 21.

Matilda Fletcher spoke to-night to the largest audience gathered here during the campaign. There was a large number of ladies present. Her speech gave the highest satisfaction to the Republicans. It was full of wit and humor, and sparkling passages, and was finely adapted to the present stage of the canvass.

Special Despatch to the St. Louis Globe.]

BURLINGTON, Iowa, October 21.

The Republicans of this city crowded Union Hall to overflowing this evening to listen to a brilliant and logical speech for Grant and Wilson, by Matilda Fletcher, who is doing great good in defence of the present Administration. Her speech was received with great applause.

[From the Burlington Hawkeye.]

We find it quite impossible to give a satisfactory synopsis even of her address. Some idea of its interest and power may be judged from the fact that she took the platform at a little before 9 o'clock, and that for nearly two hours she held the closest attention of the very large audience, a large proportion of whom were standing. Her speech was an original one, quite out of the beaten track of ordinary campaign speeches. It bristled with sharp points, eliciting repeated and enthusiastic applause, and was pervaded with a lively and mirth-provoking spirit of wit and pleasantry, which kept her hearers in the best of humor from the beginning to the end. The speech had also its more serious passages, some of which were fine specimens of argument and eloquence.   *   *   *   *   *   *

FORT MADISON.

Special Despatch to the Inter-Ocean, Chicago.]

FORT MADISON, Iowa, October 23.

The largest and by far the most enthusiastic meeting in this portion of our State was held here last evening, under the auspices of the Grant and Wilson Club. The crowd commenced to assemble early in the evening, and by the time the speaker arrived the hall was a perfect jam, a great many going home, being unable to get in. There were a great many ladies present, which added much to the enthusiasm of the meeting. At 8 o'clock Colonel Morrison introduced Matilda Fletcher, who came forward amid a storm of applause, and for nearly two hours held enthralled her large audience. Her address was clear, concise, and argumentative, and fairly bristling with wit and sarcasm.

*   *   *   *   *   *   *

[From the Fort Madison Plaindealer.]

The audience room was entirely too *strait*

last Tuesday evening. Scarcely half the assembled crowd could gain admittance, and the hall was crowded, and the stairway down to the lower hall. It was a spontaneous tribute to the reputation of the speaker, and to the cause which she represents.   *   *   *   The speech was rhetorically brilliant. It cannot be reported; it must be heard. It was an oral address—an oration, not an essay, nor an argument. The manner of the speaker is pleasant, the gesticulation easy, and graceful, the tones of voice clear and full, and the crowning glory, the ministration of comfort, the vials of consolation to the wounded and dying—not in the last ditch, but "on the home stretch," borne by "that tidal wave."

KEOKUK.

Associated Press Despatch.]

KEOKUK, Iowa, October 23.

Matilda Fletcher demonstrated her oratorical power by holding one thousand listeners in the Opera House to-night, while for two hours she dealt out a combination of sound logic and keen wit. The speech is pronounced the best of the campaign.

[From the Keokuk Gate City.]

An immense audience, composed of our very best citizens, assembled at the Opera House last night to hear Matilda Fletcher, Iowa's gifted lady orator, discuss the issues of the campaign. How well that audience was pleased in the able manner in which the lady handled her subject was indicated by the frequent and enthusiastic applause with which she was greeted. She spoke for nearly two hours, and was listened to with the very closest attention on the part of all her hearers.

It is impossible at this time to give even a brief synopsis, or to state any of the leading points, but altogether it was one of the best speeches delivered in Keokuk during the campaign, and was so pronounced by a very large number of persons who heard it, and who are fully competent to judge of its merits. It was replete not only with logical deductions, but with happy hits and keen wit as well.

OTTUMWA.

Special Despatch to the Inter-Ocean, Chicago.]

OTTUMWA, Iowa, October 24.
Matilda Fletcher, Iowa's gifted lady orator, spoke here to-night to an immense audience. She has wonderful oratorical gifts, and experiences no difficulty in holding an uncomfortably seated audience in rapt attention from the beginning to the close of a two hours' speech.

[From the Ottumwa Courier.)

MATILDA FLETCHER'S SPEECH.

This gifted lady spoke in this city last night for two hours to a very large and enthusiastic audience of ladies and gentlemen. Her speech was the fullest and most complete vindication of the President we have yet heard. She is a remarkably ready and and fluent speaker, and is perfectly at home in the current topics of the day. Her flight of eloquence when describing the grand record of the Republican party and the noble and gallant deeds of General Grant, fascinated her audience, while her keen and searching sallies of wit brought down the house again and again in storms of applause. Scores of people unable to find seats, stood up in the entrance and in the aisles and heard her throughout, and many more turned reluctantly away and left, unable to gain an admittance.

DES MOINES.

Associated Press Dispatch.]

DES MOINES, Iowa, October 24.
The largest gathering of Republicans there has been in Des Moines the present campaign assembled to-night to hear the popular woman orator of this State, Matilda Fletcher.

Governor Carpenter was the president of the meeting. The hall in which the meeting was held was crowded to its utmost capacity, and over two thousand people were turned away from the door, not being able to gain admittance. The speaker spoke for nearly two hours, dealing brilliantly with all the principal questions of the day, and discussing extensively the relative merits of the two candidates for the Presidency. The immense audience showed enthusiastic accord with it, and all present were delighted. One-half of those present were ladies who seemed especially proud of the eloquent representative of their sex.

Special Telegram to the Chicago Times.]

DES MOINES, Iowa, October 25.
An immense audience assembled this evening to hear a great speech from Matilda Fletcher. She spoke about two hours. It was one of the largest meetings of the campaign.

Special Telegram to the Inter-Ocean, Chicago.]

DES MOINES, Iowa, October 25.
Matilda Fletcher spoke here to-night to the largest and finest audience yet assembled during the campaign in this city. A large portion of the audience were ladies, and she was frequently applauded. Governor Carpenter presided as chairman.

[From the Des Moines State Register.]

Des Moines never fails to give cordial greeting to the best class of orators. Within the past and passing political campaign we have been favored with addresses from many of the most distinguished speakers of the day, and they were proud to meet the audiences that Des Moines furnished. None of them, however, have received so overwhelming a demonstration of popular favor as Matilda Fletcher did last evening. Long before the hour announced for the commencement of the meeting the hall was jammed and packed. At least one thousand people were crowded in the room. Every stationary seat was filled, and all chairs that could be wedged in were brought into service. All around the speaker, thronging the steps of the rostrum, and leaving barely room for her to stand, were gathered the finest and best audience that ever assembled at a political meeting in Des Moines. All the State officers, the business men who have given to the capital commercial prestige; the attorneys, whose reputation has made the Des Moines bar second to none in the State; the clergy, and hundreds of ladies whose social and intellectual gifts have left favorable impress on the years since Des Moines become the leading city of Iowa—all that could inspire or lend countenance or *eclat* to an address were there collected. For nearly two hours the speaker held the closest attention of the crowded and uncomfortably-seated audience —the dense throng at the doors and entrances constantly growing larger, instead of less. Applause was frequent and warm, while the absorbed attention given to every part of the speech was an indorsement still more complimentary. Governor Carpenter presided over the assembly, introducing the speaker with a glowing acknowledgment of the valuable service she had been rendering in Ohio, Indiana, and Illinois, and expressions of the just pride that Iowa feels in her efforts and name.   *   *   *

[From the Des Moines Republican.]

The largest political gathering yet assembled during the campaign met last evening to listen to the address of Matilda Fletcher. Every possible space was filled. Hundreds were obliged to stand, and hundreds were unable to get within the hall. The audience were composed of the most refined, cultivated, and educated portion of this community. It was such as would give inspiration to a speaker, and the orator, moved by the spirit of the occasion, gave one of the most brilliant and eloquent speeches yet heard by the people of this city.

CLINTON,
Associated Press Despatch.]

CLINTON, Iowa, October 29.

Matilda Fletcher's meeting in this city this evening was the finest in-door meeting of the campaign. Smith's Opera House was packed and hundreds turned away.

[From the Clinton Herald.]

So much has been said in the papers about Matilda Fletcher's oratory, and about the peculiar manner she possesses of presenting her views, that we find it difficult to write anything original. She has a fine, penetrating, but not loud, voice, the modulations of which are as delightful as music. Then she has an even flow of choice language, and an aptness in clothing her ideas possessed by only few public speakers. With her, in many instances, the concluding and emphatic word nails the sentiment irrevocably, and carries the mind of the listener captive. In this respect she resembles that greatest orator of the country, Wendell Phillips. Then she has a humorous vein which, after the enunciation of a sentiment frequently finds its culmination in a simple nod of the head or a facial expression, irresistible in its character. Of Tom Corwin it used to be said, "the drollery of his speeches consisted chiefly in the peculiar arrangement of his lineaments— that one-half the force would be lost by not seeing the man." Of Matilda Fletcher this can be said partially, as, most unexpectedly, in her discourse will a single, unstudied action give full force to the view she is elaborating. Graceful in her movements, and not given to much gesture, she holds the hearer constantly easy as to her ability to make the point at which she is aiming. In her impassioned moods she rises to the dignity of true and fervid eloquence, touching the climax without effort, and having the auditory with her unerringly.   *   *   *   *   *.   *

CEDAR RAPIDS.
[From the Cedar Rapids Times.]
MATILDA FLETCHER.

This worthily-honored lady addressed our citizens on the political issues of the day on Wednesday evening of last week in Union Opera House The house was literally crowded with ladies and gentlemen, and Matilda Fletcher did herself and cause ample justice. The campaign being over, we will not attempt a *resume* of her speech, but will say that it was a masterly effort, and one which would have done credit to the intellect of the best masculine stump-speakers in the field. Her manner is easy, graceful, and pleasing. Her speech was a *manly* one from *womanly* lips—strong, forcible, and conclusive—delighting her audience, and leading her hearers along through various gradations of argument, wit, sarcasm, and eulogy, so easily and naturally that two hours sped by without the least sign of weariness from any one.

[From the Cedar Rapids Republican.]

The announcement that Matilda Fletcher would discuss the political issues of the day in Union Opera House last night, brought out an immense audience of the *elite* of the city. Long before she arrived the dress and parquette circles and gallery of the Opera House were literally crowded with ladies and gentlemen, who were anxious to hear this gifted lady orator. She spoke for nearly two hours, and held the audience spell-bound, except when the stillness was broken by applause. Her style is easy and graceful ; her rhetoric above criticism ; her voice full and enunciation clear, and her manner of handling political questions is at once dignified and pungent. Her entire lecture was a net-work of facts, so connected and well applied as to frequently elicit the hearty applause of the audience.

 * * * * * * *

DUBUQUE.
Special Despatch to the Inter-Ocean, Chicago.]

DUBUQUE, Iowa, October 31.

Matilda Fletcher addressed the largest political gathering of the campaign here this evening. The hall was crowded to overflowing, and many were unable to gain admission. She made a rousing speech, which was cordially welcomed by frequent and warm applause. Her defence of the Administration was logical and masterly, giving universal satisfaction, and cannot but have a good effect.

[From the Dubuque Times.]

Dubuque is not sure to give a cordial welcome to the best orators. She is a little inclined to pay homage to notabilities from abroad, and leave equally able talent belonging to her own State unappreciated. But our city did honor to itself as well as to the speaker by the generous welcome and cordial greeting which she last evening gave Matilda Fletcher, the Iowa poet and orator, and the orator was worthy of the occasion. * * * * * *

SIOUX CITY.
Associated Press Despatch.]

SIOUX CITY, Iowa, November 4.

The campaign closed here to-night with a stirring address by Matilda Fletcher to a large audience.

[From the Sioux City Journal.]

Notwithstanding a dark and disagreeable night, with streets so heavy with mud and walks so slippery with earthern paste that pedestrianism was both difficult and dangerous, the Academy was filled last night by the largest and best audience of the campaign to listen to Matilda Fletcher, the woman of Iowa. The finest ladies of the town braved the night and gathered numerously to do honor to a sister who has done so much to honor herself and ennobl< and dignify her sex. Under all the circumstances, we can truthfully say that Sioux City never had so successful a public meeting, political or other, and we may say further that it was a deserved tribute to a deserving woman and a noble cause.

Matilda Fletcher has been speaking continuously for many weeks, visiting Nebraska, New York, Michigan, Ohio, Indiana, and Illinois, in all of which States she met the same unbounded success that attended the close of her campaign labors in Sioux City last night. And after weeks of such exhausting labor, it will strike many that she appeared remarkably fresh, that her voice was singularly unimpaired, and that altogether she seemed to have held up amazingly—for a woman. But when we add that she was astir at 5 o'clock yesterday morning ; that she came through from Fort Dodge on a freight train in order to meet her appointment here ; that she had fasted until 5 o'clock in the evening; that she had only time after reaching the hotel to get her tea and prepare for the meeting, and that she appeared promptly on time, and entertained that large audience for nearly two hours, we think all men will agree with us, and heartily agree, that a woman is not necessarily the delicate, helpless thing that some—Dr. Bushnell included—have been pleased to picture her.

And Matilda Fletcher did not appear masculine, or coarse, or aught else than a womanly woman, and a handsome woman, on the platform of the Academy, by any means, and as any man whose judgment is worthy will bear us testimony. In her dress, in her manner, in the tone of her voice, in all or either, there was no sacrifice as we could see of any attribute of womanly modesty or womanly grace.

Of her address we cannot speak at length, much as we should like to. We should say, coming from a man, that it was able, that it was thoughtful, that it was logical, that it was well connected, that it was sparkling with wit, that it was studded with great truths, that it was altogether entertaining—

and why we should not say the same, coming as it did from a woman, we cannot for the life of us see.

This we do know, if we know anything of the pulse of a public assemblage, that her hearers were greatly delighted, interested to a higher degree than they have been at any political meeting of the campaign, though the meetings have been numerous and the gentlemanly debators among the ablest of the land.

There were many no doubt who went to hear her out of pure curiosity, and if so, we are glad, because not only was their curiosity satisfied, but at the same time they listened to an eloquent and forcible speech, replete with the most substantial and incontrovertible truth this singular campaign has developed.

At the close thanks were returned to the speaker and emphasized in three hearty cheers. After this a number of ladies and gentlemen went upon the platform and personally congratulated the little woman who had captivated the personal good will of everybody present.

TO LECTURE MANAGERS.

Those desirous of securing the lectures of Matilda Fletcher will please address her agent, who has the exclusive right to make engagements. Her name does not appear on the list of any literary bureau, nor is she in any way connected with them.

Committees will please make early application that routes may be arranged with as little travel and expense as possible.

Ten days before she is to appear, a notification will be sent, telling you whence she will come, and where she will go from your place.

Telegrams must invariably be prepaid.

MARINER J. KENT, *Agent,*

P. O. Box 447, Washington, D. C.

EDITORIAL FRIENDS will confer a favor by calling attention to MATILDA FLETCHER's *Lyceum Magazine,* subjects of lectures, &c.; also, please place it in the hands of lecture committees or others interested in lectures.